What do you EXPECT?

- Executive Edition -

EXPECT LEADERSHIP

An Overview of the EXPECT LEADERSHIP Series

Written by

KEITH MARTINO

CMI Assessments
P.O. Box 703803
Dallas, TX 75370-3803
www.CMIAssessments.com

EXPECT LEADERSHIP

What if...

You defined **"Leadership"** in your company
as the ability to impact others through
positive influence?

◆

Consider the possibilities...

If each of your employees believed
they could demonstrate **"Leadership"** daily
regardless of their position or title.

◆

Imagine the benefits if...

You introduced your employees to a simple
"Leadership" model that enables every one to proactively
solve problems before they erupt into a firestorm.

"Expect, Understand, and Own the Positive Future!"

In this Executive Edition of *EXPECT LEADERSHIP*
you will come to appreciate the powerful concept
behind each of these words.

◆

It will encourage you to prepare your employees
to demonstrate stronger leadership
beginning today.

◆

And provide a scalable model
that will enhance your company's performance
and change your employees' lives forever.

Expect Leadership

- Executive Edition -

Table of Contents

A Moment of Truth
Can Blindside any CEO
or Executive

Never Fear -
Your most catastrophic challenges can
yield surprisingly positive outcomes when you
Expect, Understand and Own the Positive Future!

Agile LeadersThink Fast!

The golf cart came roaring down the hill!

Near the bottom of the ravine stood Jacque, a sharp, young IT professional. He was entertaining a handful of his firm's best clients. Jacque was frozen in place and too stunned to speak. His last thought, "Surely he wouldn't run me over." Then the lights went out. Too late! His "buddy" had flattened him at full speed.

The next thing Jacque remembered, he was opening his eyes in the recovery room. The surgeon announced Jacque had a broken femur. His leg would likely never be the same. Jacque's mind raced with a lot of questions. How could this happen? What would he do to support his family? How could he recover his soaring medical expenses?

Jacque's solution... Sue the golf course! Sure. He had to do something!

Trevor, the firm's CEO and Founder, sat across the table from me a short while later explaining the incident. Trevor was equally traumatized. It was their Annual Customer Appreciation Golf Tournament. An unnamed employee had taken full advantage of the open bar Trevor had arranged primarily for clients. After a few brewskies, it occurred to this unnamed employee that it might be funny to give one of his colleagues a scare. After all, what could go wrong?

So, he pointed his cart at his teammate and took off with full confidence. Obviously, Jacque would jump out of the way. Jacque's last thought, "Surely he wouldn't run me over."

Now Trevor was on the verge of potentially losing his company due to the horseplay of a half-drunken programmer. He wasn't about to let it happen again. He was heartbroken, but as a leader, Trevor was fleet-footed.

As Trevor shared his story, I was reminded how quickly we must think and act as leaders.

In order to host the tournament, Trevor had signed a contract with the golf course. It included a clause whereby Trevor had accepted full responsibility for anything that happened at the event. Golf course management was not worried.

How would he save his company? How would he take good care of his valuable employees? How would he ensure this never happened again?

Trevor was facing a *Moment of Truth*.

WHAT IS A MOMENT OF TRUTH (MOT)?

No matter how large or small the team you lead, a *Moment of Truth* will find you. You'll be greeted with challenges and circumstances you can't control. Your reputation will be at stake. And no matter how coolly you play your cards, your emotions and blood pressure will soar!

So, what is a *Moment of Truth*?
A *Moment of Truth* is that untimely instant when you realize that there is an accelerating problem of seemingly epic proportion. You must make a quick decision under unpleasant conditions. You have incomplete information. Your welfare and the welfare of others are at risk. And yes, your entire team is watching. That's a *Moment of Truth.*

Ouch! So who's to blame?
You? Your boss? Your employees? Your customers?
Perhaps all of the above. Consider everyone a suspect. *Yourself included.*

No single individual will be entirely at fault. You'll soon discover that many of your friends, colleagues or even family accidentally contributed to the mess despite their best intentions. There will be no "one throat to choke." Instead, there will be plenty of blame to spread around. And for you as the leader, the downside will be painfully obvious.

Moments of Truth are simple to describe. They're hard to handle!

But, from whence do they come?
Often weeks, months or years of neglect culminate toward this calamity we call a *Moment of Truth.* Usually, everyone looks the other way while an emerging issue is brewing. Then at the least desirable moment that pesky issue crosses through a tipping point. Suddenly it picks up speed and quickly digresses into an overnight catastrophe. Everyone... and no one... saw it coming.

Here's the good news!
The *Executive Edition* of EXPECT LEADERSHIP contains three real world scenarios where someone is facing a *Moment of Truth.* It could be you or a peer. This book is designed to help you and your team practice a consistently successful technique for resolving any *Moment of Truth* successfully.

When you practice the five simple steps described in this book, you can survive and thrive under the toughest of circumstances.

Expect, Understand and Own the Positive Future!

*A Moment of Truth
Can Strike At Any Level in a Business...
Even at the Frontlines.*

Keep in mind –
A frontline employee's most catastrophic moments
can also yield surprisingly positive outcomes.

EXPECT LEADERSHIP

AN EARLY MEMORY

I'll admit it. I was desperate.

As the new Xerox Commercial Print Rep, I needed to close a deal. Badly! The year was off to a painfully slow start.

Some sales-guru guy on CD had quipped, "Just make ONE more call per day on your way home. You'll exceed your goals." So here I was. It was 5:00 p.m. and I was driving up to a dilapidated building. The marquee read Quick Printer - just a sloppy sign barely hanging on. Kinda like me. But what did I have to lose?" I hadn't YET met the Kearneys. Yikes!

Old man Kearney (as they called him) greeted me at the front counter. He growled "What-do-you-want?" It wasn't the best way to begin a sales call, but that's why they call it perseverance, right? I got straight to the point. He needed a Xerox High-Speed Duplicator to rejuvenate his business. He got straight to a different point. "Young man, you should leave and never come back." That would have actually been good advice, if I'd only listened.

I'm sorry to say, I saw his challenge as an open invitation. Learning to qualify a prospect was something I would master later in my career. For now, Mr. Kearney was in my cross-hairs.

Once I was safely into the Kearneys' shop, they pulled down the shades and we cut a deal. It was simple. I would help them find a large printing job, supply all the paper and toner, provide the sophisticated equipment and help their son Lee complete the work. Then they would sign my agreement. Done.

The next day before I could rethink my hasty decision, Lee called with the good news. They had found a really big job. It was available for that evening. Looks like we were in business!

It was truly a BIG job. No lie. When Lee came to the corporate office that evening, I was stunned at the magnitude of supplies it would consume. We had just started with the work when Lee announced that he wouldn't be around long. After all, it was bowling night.

I learned a lot that evening. In the quiet of an otherwise empty building, I learned how demanding it can be to carry dozens of cases of paper down the hall without a two-wheeler. I learned how fast you can deplete a supply closet. I learned sales is not an easy career.

Lee showed up bright and early the next morning. He waved as he drove off in his pickup truck with a promise to call me ASAP. The call never came. The Kearneys took an extended vacation to Florida. I suppose they had a good time. They never ordered the Xerox machine.

How would I salvage my pride in the eyes of my peers? How would I pay for the paper that job consumed? How would I win a multitude of contests and ultimately earn the Xerox President's Club status?

I realized that I was facing a *Moment of Truth.*

A Moment of Truth
Can Debilitate a Team and
Cripple Key Relationships.

On the Other Hand –
Your team's most catastrophic moments can
yield surprisingly positive results.

EXPECT LEADERSHIP

You Know Your Team is Facing a Moment of Truth When...

Your largest customer threatens to cancel their multi-year contract because your vendor shipped to the wrong address... again!

Your delivery team is cutting corners on a top account, resulting in higher profits and a bonus for everyone (including yourself).

An auditor discovered your top supplier has been overcharging you for years.

Your IT team has taken on strategic significance in your company and you're realizing as an IT Director that you can't be everywhere.

A senior project manager made a commitment he didn't keep.

Now your company's ERP initiative is running behind and your company is losing orders!

- FIVE STEPS -
TO A BRIGHTER FUTURE

"Expect, Understand and Own the Positive Future!"

| **Expect** | | **Understand** | **and Own** | **the Positive** | **Future** |
| A better outcome than if the problem had never occurred. | | Ask open-ended questions. Understand perceptions. | Take ownership by apologizing or thanking others. | Remain positive... as a matter of principle! | Create a plan and make it happen! |

Five Steps to a Better Solution
In Your Moment of Truth

EXPECT, UNDERSTAND and OWN
the POSITIVE FUTURE!

Repeat these five steps and solve a tough challenge:

1. Expect

2. Understand

3. Own

4. Positive

5. Future

Step 1

EXPECT
Envision and communicate a better outcome than if the problem had never occurred.

To initiate the thought process... Expect means:

1) Envision the ideal end result.

2) Ensure It's the best potential outcome for all parties.

3) Communicate your expectation to your peers.

1. Expect -
A better outcome than if the problem had never occurred.

Do we typically spring into a catastrophe expecting and seeking a better outcome from the event than if it had never occurred? Not likely. It's hard for many of us to find the silver lining amidst the chaos. Just as importantly, do we communicate a "better than ever" expectation to the involved parties? Usually not.

Notice these Nuances:
- Real enthusiasm is contagious.
- Most people tend to cast low or unrealistic expectations.
- High expectations generally require greater effort and a change in perspective.
- The true character of your team is on display when you raise expectations.
- Speed is essential. The faster you recast team expectations the better.

Tips for Setting Expectations:
- Involve your peers, superiors and customers in the expectation setting process.
- Discuss the impact of the ideal expectations on each member of the team.
- Exude authentic confidence. Choose your tone of voice carefully. Stay real.
- Clear your mind and energize your countenance prior to delivering your message.
- Proactively seek counsel from a positive mentor or proven achiever if possible.

Landmines to Avoid:
- Never say something you don't believe to be true.
- Ensure that every person involved weighs in with their perspective.
- Discuss key points until you have a commitment from key parties.

Expect
A better outcome than if the problem had never occurred.

Understand
Ask open-ended questions. Understand perceptions.

Step 2

UNDERSTAND
Ask open-ended questions.
Understand perceptions and WHY.

Examples:

- What happened from your perspective?

- How do you feel about this issue?

- What were the consequences to our relationship?

- What do you believe contributed to this situation?

- How do you think we should handle this challenge?

2. Understand -
Ask open-ended questions.
Understand perceptions and WHY.

When faced with calamity, do we seek to understand? Or, are we quick to blame? For most of us, it's not intuitive to ask rational questions in an emotional moment. We may believe we already understand the situation. Yet, the empathy we acquire once we begin asking questions brings clarity. Often, it explains "why" someone did what they did. The "why" is what's important for building a plan.

Notice these Nuances:
- Emotions blind our senses and cause us to become insular in our thinking.
- Our vantage point is often limited by our role or position in the organization.
- In our haste to resolve the perceived challenge, we often overlook feelings.
- Sincerely seeking to understand is a powerful way to show we care.
- Solving the immediate problem will not ensure the enthusiasm of the team.

Tips for Understanding Others:
- Ask the difficult questions even if it feels uncomfortable.
- Consider the intensity with which each person expresses his opinion.
- Probe about the priority of each concern raised to determine its relative importance.
- Prepare a list of questions in advance if possible. It will free you to listen more closely.
- Demonstrate a genuine curiosity for how people feel and why they feel as they do.

Landmines to Avoid:
- Conflict avoidance is deadly.
- Be willing to face the reality of how others perceive the issues.
- Be prepared to adjust our perspective somewhat as we acknowledge others' views.
- Resist the temptation to proceed too quickly. Hear the perspectives of others.
- Take adequate time to reflect on perspectives. Hasty responses damage trust.
- Keep your cool no matter what is shared. Focus on reaching the expectation.

| **Expect**
A better outcome than if the problem had never occurred. | **Understand**
Ask open-ended questions. Understand perceptions. | **and Own**
Take ownership by apologizing or thanking others. | | |

Step 3

and OWN
Take ownership by apologizing or thanking others.

Examples – PICK ONE.

To take ownership of the future direction:

1) Say "I apologize" for:

    a. "Not acting quickly enough."

    b. "Not having spoken out sooner."

    c. "Not bringing it to your attention earlier."

2) Say "Thank you" for:

    a. "Sharing your perspective with me."

    b. "Your honesty in dealing with this matter."

    c. "Your leadership under these difficult circumstances."

3. Own –
Take ownership by apologizing or thanking others.

This step is difficult for some. Learning to sincerely apologize when we have made a mistake is tough. Apologizing when we intentionally did the wrong thing can be excruciatingly painful, but needed. And it's seldom easy to thank a person for their candor when told something we do not want to hear.

Notice these Nuances:
- The act of verbalizing a simple, sincere apology is becoming a lost art.
- The admission of having made a mistake is NOT the same as expressing an apology.
- The acknowledgement of someone's actions is NOT the same as saying "thank you."
- Often the lack of an apology or sincere thanks undermines the relationship potential.
- A sincere apology or word of thanks can turbocharge many relationships.
- If your words and actions are inconsistent, people believe your actions.

Tips for Apologizing or Thanking Others:
- Demonstrate sincerity through your words and actions.
- Focus on the long term viability of the relationship.
- Avoid (to the best of your ability) making the same mistakes again.
- Notice the positive things your peers are doing and overlook their negative actions.
- Be the first to recognize success and express your thanks.

Landmines to Avoid:
- Failing to say "I apologize" simply because your pride is at risk.
- Failing to say "thank you" simply because your pride is at risk.
- Failing to say "thank you" because it has already been expressed by someone else.
- Failing to say "I apologize" because you feel you have also been wronged.
- Skipping over this ESSENTIAL step because you believe it is not needed.

| **Expect** | **Understand** | **and Own** | **the Positive** | |
| A better outcome than if the problem had never occurred. | Ask open-ended questions. Understand perceptions. | Take ownership by apologizing or thanking others. | Remain positive... as a matter of principle! | |

Step 4

the POSITIVE
Remain positive
and introduce your principles.

Two Suggestions:

1) No matter what you've learned from the conversation so far, remain positive.

2) Now is the time to introduce your company's core principles into the conversation.

4. Positive –
Remain positive
and introduce your principles.

Remaining positive in the face of "Understanding" and "Owning" the situation can be the key to unlocking the best potential solution. But it doesn't always seem logical to maintain a positive attitude. This book is based on ten positive principles mentioned below. Your company may have a set of values or principles. If not, use the principles shown below.

Notice these Nuances:
- Human emotions can be volatile. Practice discipline and remain positive.

- Successful leaders embrace proven principles that steady their resolve.

- Effective leaders spotlight the principles that guide their words and actions.

Tips for Remaining Positive.
- Practice and mention these Principles* in difficult conversations.

  1. Demonstrate Integrity
  2. Lead by Example
  3. Address Challenges One-on-One
  4. Be Proactive
  5. Reinforce Transparency
  6. Encourage Others
  7. Motivate with Passion!
  8. Deliver Solutions
  9. Create Milestones
  10. Improve Daily

Landmines to Avoid:
- Failing to embrace a solid set of principles that you know are on target.

*Each of these ten principles is explained more fully
in the *EXPECT LEADERSHIP* Journal.

Expect	**Understand**	**and Own**	**the Positive**		**Future**
A better outcome than if the problem had never occurred.	Ask open-ended questions. Understand perceptions.	Take ownership by apologizing or thanking others.	Remain positive... as a matter of principle!		Create a plan and make it happen!

Step 5

FUTURE
Create a plan:

a. Action Items

b. Who's Responsible?

c. Due Dates

And make it happen!

The future gets better when we:

1. Establish a game plan that is achievable and agreeable.

2. Develop specific next steps (action items).

3. Discuss who is responsible for each action item.

4. Agree to a timeline for completion of the action items.

5. Make the plan happen. Adjust the plan as needed.

5. Future –
Create a plan,
and make it happen!

Our natural tendency is to jump into action before thinking through the development of a plan. Each of these steps challenges our fight or flight instincts. These steps tell us to hang in there and solve the problem while preserving the relationship.

Notice these Nuances:
- People tend to jump to the solution step too early. It's a deceptive trap.
- Many problems are resolved in a manner that leaves relationships in shambles.
- The solution to any catastrophe should solve problems AND preserve relationships.
- Focusing on the solution prematurely is a perilous approach (at best).
- Often meetings end before we develop action items. This is an ominous signal.

Tips for Developing a Plan to: *Expect, Understand and Own the Positive Future!*
- Review the ideal outcome again before you begin the planning process.
- Develop a list of questions that remain unresolved. Ask these questions ASAP.
- Apologize for any mistakes made. Thank those who have made a positive impact.
- Ensure that everyone is in a positive mindset by introducing key principles.
- Develop a solid plan with action items, responsible parties and due dates.

Landmines to Avoid:
- Settling for a plan that leaves issues unresolved and/or relationships damaged.
- Establishing a feedback process that is lax and unresponsive to change.
- Failing to repeat all steps in the process if the solution is not accomplished quickly.
- Missing the opportunity to build a stronger team as you resolve the target issue.
- Allowing a problem to linger because it is deemed too difficult to resolve.

LET'S TALK
ABOUT THE FUTURE!

How can we survive
a *Moment of Truth* and be "better off
than if it had never occurred?"

"BETTER OFF THAN IF IT HAD NEVER OCCURRED" WHAT DOES THAT MEAN?

Do we believe dealing with a Moment of Truth is always pleasant? No way. Thankfully, it's often easier than expected. But sometimes it's more painful than a root canal. Either way, you know when you've reached that fork in the road and you have to make a crucial decision. That's when you take a deep breath, collect your wits and remember this model - *Expect, Understand and Own the Positive Future!*

But, let's be clear. We're not suggesting that everyone will always be delighted with the short term outcome. That may not be an achievable goal. This is especially true if certain individuals created the problem you must resolve. Perfection may not be within reach. Improvement is! You may not be able to guarantee every single relationship will be "good as new" when the dust settles. However, when you and your friends, family or colleagues look back at the big picture, if you *Expect, Understand and Own the Positive Future!* you will be better off than if the situation had never occurred.

For instance... If an employee stole a customer's laptop, it may be necessary to terminate the employee, press charges, establish new procedures, restore the customer's loss and advise all employees of the new inventory management system. However, the ex-employee might not be happy.

IT DOES **NOT** MEAN...

Everyone is delighted.

Perfection has been reached.

You should stop working to improve the situation.

Each relationship is "as good as new."

When you EXPECT LEADERSHIP:

You activate the unrealized potential for growth inside each person.

◆

You equip them with a fresh mindset.

◆

And –

Your employees' most catastrophic challenges can be turned into surprisingly positive outcomes at work and at home.

PREPARE YOUR TEAM
BEFORE DISASTER
STRIKES!

The next three real word MOT examples illustrate the versatility of the five step model in solving challenges before they career out of control. If left unchecked, the implications are deadly. Most companies don't get nuked. They bleed profits from a thousand preventable cuts. That should not be your story. *EXPECT LEADERSHIP* at all levels.

The following MOT examples also reflect our suggested training approach. In each instance role playing is highly recommended to ensure employees retain key concepts.

In MOT #1 – *EXPECT LEADERSHIP.* Your team will avoid losing customers, risking revenue and ruining your reputation.

In MOT #2 – *EXPECT LEADERSHIP.* Those data security processes you put in place to avoid calamity will pay major dividends.

In MOT #3 – *EXPECT LEADERSHIP.* Employee retention will rise while turnover will be reduced – especially in key areas.

The purpose of using these frontline *Moment of Truth* examples is to remind everyone of this important point: Even seemingly basic issues (in the absence of someone stepping up and demonstrating leadership) will ultimately lead to an executive level *Moment of Truth*. Eliminate the drama. EXPECT LEADERSHIP on the frontlines.

The Customer Notices Lagging Enthusiasm
MOT Challenge #1

Scenario:

Management asked Justin to lead a major project for one of your largest clients. While he was initially quite enthusiastic, he soon lost interest in seeing the project through to completion. Everyone including the customer noticed!

Challenge:

Key individuals showed up late for project related meetings. Justin never seemed to be concerned. The level of expectation among team members was dropping like a rock. Furthermore, Justin was beginning to make excuses for his group's lack of initiative. Lately, Justin has begun blaming the customer for expecting too much... and paying too little.

You are a recognized leader within your company. You realize leadership is a daily expectation.

Key Question:

As Justin's peer, how will you handle this situation?

MOT Challenge #1

A Timely Opportunity
for Justin's Co-worker to
Expect, Understand and Own the Positive Future!

To save the client relationship and invigorate the team, let's *EXPECT LEADERSHIP*.

EXPECT LEADERSHIP: As Justin's peer, you will be encouraged to step in and:

- Focus the team on delivering a positive outcome for your customer.
- Ask the right questions to uncover critical perspectives and input.
- Express apologies as needed. Thank those who are performing well.
- Refocus the team in a positive direction by interjecting core values.
- Prompt a planning event that creates fresh action items, responsible parties and a realistic and acceptable timeline.

Remember –
This team's most catastrophic moments can
yield surprisingly positive outcomes.

The Customer Notices Lagging Enthusiasm

1 **2** **3**

MOT Challenge #1 - Our Solution

Expect
A better outcome than if the problem had never occurred.

#1 – EXPECT and communicate the ideal outcome:
- Deliver the customer's project with excellence.
- Ensure the team leader delivers on a new positive, constructive game plan.
- Put a process in place to ensure the quality of future projects.

Understand
Ask open-ended questions. Understand perceptions.

#2 – UNDERSTAND the situation. Ask your colleagues what happened:
- Ensure you understand how the project leader feels about the project status.
- Understand this project leader's level of motivation and commitment.
- Assess if it is possible for this leader to rapidly improve this scenario.

and Own
Take ownership by apologizing or thanking others.

#3 – OWN the outcome. Demonstrate leadership:
- Thank the project leader for sharing his/her candid feelings.
- Apologize for not offering to help earlier.

the Positive
Remain positive... as a matter of principle!

#4 – Accelerate POSITIVE leadership momentum:
- Explain that you (as a company teammate) are also a resource to help.
- Contribute positive energy and encouragement. Strategize with the leader.
- Explain how company principles of customer service apply in this scenario.
- Encourage other team members to help get the project back on track.
- Escalate the situation if the leader is not demonstrating urgency.

Future
Create a plan and make it happen!

#5 – Plan for the FUTURE. Help others reach the ideal expectation:
- Re-establish action items for the team members to get the project on track.
- Ensure each team member recommits to their revised action items.
- Gain commitment for an acceptable date for each action item.
- Ensure the customer is aware of the new game plan and the renewed commitment to deliver an outstanding service on time and on budget.
- Follow up to ensure the project moves forward and achieves success.

You've Worked
AROUND the Process
MOT Challenge #2

Scenario:

Your IT department has recently implemented a series of new processes to avoid the loss of sensitive data. Management now requires everyone to use these new procedures for key activities.

You attended the meetings where the planning took place. You quietly went along with the proposed recommendations. You never mentioned you didn't agree with the way the company developed and documented the new processes. Now you believe these new procedures aren't working.

On the last two projects, you've worked around the new processes to get your portion of each job completed on time and on budget. No one seems to have noticed that you haven't been following the guidelines. You believe you completed these projects to the customer's satisfaction.

Challenge:

Everyone believes you are following approved processes to get these jobs completed. You have two choices. Keep doing things the way you've been doing them and hope that no one finds out. Or you can address the issues you have with the currently approved processes.

You'd like to keep doing what you've been doing. But deep down you don't feel good about it.

Key Question:

How will you handle this situation?

MOT Challenge #2

It's Not Too Late for this Employee to
Expect, Understand and Own the Positive Future!

Even though this employee has let the company down, *EXPECT LEADERSHIP.*

EXPECT LEADERSHIP to establish a culture where employees feel compelled to:

- Refocus their energies on delivering positive outcomes despite mistakes.
- Ask questions to uncover how the processes they skipped over may have impacted others.
- Apologize as needed, and thank those who provide insight.
- Recommit in a positive way to your company's core values.
- Identify next steps, responsible parties and a clear timeline.

Remember –
This employee's most unfortunate actions can
yield surprising process improvements.

You've Worked AROUND the Process

MOT Challenge #2 - Our Solution

Expect
A better outcome than if the problem had never occurred.

#1 – EXPECT and communicate the ideal outcome:
- Customers receive consistent, high quality solutions from your company.
- All departments are on the same page regarding the approved processes.
- You act with integrity by following the process as agreed.
- All data is secure.

Understand
Ask open-ended questions. Understand perceptions.

#2 – UNDERSTAND the situation. Ask your colleagues what happened:
- Talk with your manager about the approved process.
- Understand the intended purpose of each step in the procedure.
- Ask management about how a "lack of follow-through" would impact others.
- Ask management for advice on when and how to handle exceptions.

and Own
Take ownership by apologizing or thanking others.

#3 – OWN the outcome. Demonstrate leadership:
- Apologize for failing to present your concerns about the process earlier.
- Apologize for bypassing the approved process and for not telling anyone.

the Positive
Remain positive... as a matter of principle!

#4 – Accelerate POSITIVE leadership momentum:
- Keep an open mind about the processes and focus on the benefits.
- Respectfully communicate any lingering concerns about the process.
- Offer alternative process options that might make the process better.
- Commit to following or helping revise the approved procedures.
- Offer to work overtime to go back and repair any damage done or steps missed in your earlier projects.

Future
Create a plan and make it happen!

#5 – Plan for the FUTURE. Help others reach the ideal expectation:
- Commit to following the approved procedure for everyone's benefit.
- Report back to management on your next project how you completed all the steps of the approved processes.
- Encourage others to follow the procedure with integrity and secure the data.
- Encourage others to bring up any concerns proactively.

Weak Performance Reviews Bite Back!
MOT Challenge #3

Scenario:

You sent out a performance review packet to your direct reports. You asked each employee to respond to a series of thought-provoking questions regarding their own performance.

You asked each employee to list:

- Three of their most significant accomplishments.
- Two areas where they fell short.
- One improvement step they can take immediately.

You are pleased because you know each person had some good things to document. On the other hand, you also know there are areas in each person's performance where they need to improve.

Challenge:

Historically, you've felt you should be upbeat with every employee despite their performance. As a result, you've avoided discussing the tough issues. You realize the prior review process wasn't as helpful as it could have been. In addition, you didn't address several issues because you would have been uncomfortable discussing negative topics. You have already lost a couple of your top performers.

Today is the day you provide feedback to your team. Your first direct report comes into your office for feedback. His performance is okay, but not great. You're thinking about the need for candor as he enters.

Key Question:

As a manager, how will you handle this situation?

MOT Challenge #3

It's Time for this Manager to
Expect, Understand and Own the Positive Future!

EXPECT LEADERSHIP in your company and improve frontline coaching as leaders:

- Deliver performance reviews that benefit the employee and company.
- Prompt employees to share how they feel about their role and contribution.
- Extend thanks to those who consistently deliver outstanding results.
- Offer positive, candid and respectful critique to those who need direction.
- Conduct a regular planning event that provides feedback, identifies developmental steps, and a clear timeline for completion.

Remember –
Even a manager's most unfortunate decisions can yield surprisingly positive coaching improvements.

Weak Performance Reviews Bite Back!

1 2 3

Sample Training Illustration

MOT Challenge #3 - Our Solution

Expect
A better outcome than if the problem had never occurred.

#1 – EXPECT and communicate the ideal outcome:
- Each employee has a written synopsis of what s/he has done well.
- Each employee has a written game plan for improving his/her performance.
- Each employee achieves his/her goals and knows that you are supportive.

Understand
Ask open-ended questions. Understand perceptions.

#2 – UNDERSTAND the situation. Ask your colleagues what happened:
- Meet with each employee.
- Ask each person to share how they feel about their impact on team results.

and Own
Take ownership by apologizing or thanking others.

#3 – OWN the outcome. Demonstrate leadership:
- Thank each employee for their candid appraisal of their performance.
- Apologize for having been scant on past opportunities for improvement.

the Positive
Remain positive... as a matter of principle!

#4 – Accelerate POSITIVE leadership momentum:
- Provide a strong confirmation of the good things s/he has done to date.
- Respectfully explain where s/he has fallen below expectation.
- Commit to providing accurate, helpful and productive PRs in the future.
- You may want to provide a blank PR (in advance of the meeting) to enable each person to give a comprehensive and thoughtful response.
- Ensure you mention key strengths and improvement opportunities.

Future
Create a plan and make it happen!

#5 – Plan for the FUTURE. Help others reach the ideal expectation:
- Provide a set of constructive recommendations for improvement.
- Create a game plan for these recommended action items.
- Designate a period of time in which s/he should achieve each item.
- Meet at a predetermined time in the future to measure his/her progress.

AND NOW FOR THE
REST OF THE STORY...

AGILE LEADERS THINK FAST!
HOW DID IT TURN OUT?

As you may recall, the golf cart came roaring down the hill!

Near the bottom of the ravine stood Jacque, a sharp, young IT professional. He was entertaining a handful of his firm's best clients. Jacque was frozen in place and too stunned to speak. His last thought, "Surely he wouldn't run me over." Then the lights went out. Too late! His "buddy" had flattened him at full speed.

Where we left off at page eleven, Trevor, his CEO was facing a *Moment of Truth.* How would he save his company? How would he take good care of his valuable employees? How would he ensure this never happened again?

Trevor *made the decision to EXPECT LEADERSHIP* from every one of his employees. He decided to implement *Expect, Understand and Own the Positive Future!* Here's how.

EXPECT
It wasn't easy, but Trevor would not give up hope. His determination was astounding. Trevor rapidly set his sights on getting his company back on track in a way it couldn't be so easily derailed. He vowed to himself that never again would he be in this place simply due to his own inaction. Now, Trevor's expectation is for every member of his team to feel committed to the company's future.

UNDERSTAND
Fortunately, Trevor had some good friends who were also business owners. He immediately sought their counsel about a means of strengthening the leadership at every level in his company. In his quest to fully understand how to lead his company in a turnaround, one of our clients referred Trevor to our firm. We developed a written plan, and he got it!

and OWN
Trevor courageously apologized to the injured employee in a personal visit to the hospital. He was overwhelmingly thankful when the employee graciously agreed to work with Trevor's insurance company to find a solution. As Trevor decided to own the situation, they were able to reach agreement. His heartfelt apology was central to that breakthrough.

the POSITIVE
Trevor adopted a set of principles provided by Keith Martino Leadership. He stunned us all by ordering a wall sized graphic display spotlighting the principles and the definitions of each. You couldn't miss the massive, three dimensional values Trevor posted throughout the office. Then he began a three year training endeavor that rapidly shaped the positive direction of this new culture. A few employees balked, but Trevor was not to be deterred. Eventually he chose to replace those holdouts.

FUTURE!
Trevor met the objectives he targeted. His company was rewarded by a major software provider as Partner of the Year. This was an unexpected surprise delivered by the CEO of this Fortune 100 Company during an awards dinner. Today, Trevor's company is recognized as a leader in his field. And Trevor continues to challenge his employees on a daily basis to EXPECT LEADERSHIP from each member of the team.

AN EARLY MEMORY
HOW DID IT TURN OUT?

Once I was safely into the Kearneys' raggedy old print shop, they pulled down the shades and we cut a deal. It was simple. I would help them find a large printing job, supply all the paper and toner, provide the sophisticated equipment and help their son Lee complete the work. Then they would sign my agreement.

You may remember when we left off around page thirteen, yours truly, the rookie Xerox Sales Professional and future author of this book was facing a *Moment of Truth.*

Sure, Lee had shown up bright and early the next morning. He was happy as a lark! He waved as he drove off in his pickup with a promise to call. The phone call never came. The Kearneys took an extended vacation to Florida. And of course, they never ordered the Xerox machine.

Perhaps out of the necessity to survive, I decided to implement *Expect, Understand and Own the Positive Future!* How did it shape my career? Profoundly!

EXPECT
I began a renewed pursuit for success. My target became those successful business owners on the West Coast who had demonstrated an appreciation for Xerox high-speed duplicators. My expectations were heightened by the wave of copy shops opening rapidly across the country. I felt that I could ride the wave. But, it would require a different prospect type and mindset.

UNDERSTAND
I began to make a series of phone calls to the largest copy shop franchise owners in the nation. Todd, a Kinko's Copy Shop franchisee was the first to accept my call. I asked him all sorts of questions to gain understanding of this industry. I also asked other questions like what it would take for Todd to open multiple shops in my hometown. This was a natural outflow from my new expectations.

and OWN
Todd's insight into the true nature of a high-speed copy shop was tremendously enlightening. At this point, I owned this developing relationship born out of resetting my expectations. I thanked him for his transparency and interest in considering our local market.

the POSITIVE
Then the work began. It was relatively easy compared to the past attempts. And as I met with real estate professionals to scope out potential copy shop locations, my confidence rose. The positive drive kept me moving forward and I adopted a sales principle that remains central to my work today. It is defined as "find the man, the money and the motive."

FUTURE!
Todd rapidly opened his first Kinko's Copy Shop in our city. The momentum from his large copier purchase paved the path. I developed a plan to find other copy shop owners who would move into our market. It became easier and easier to convince them as I executed this plan. Ultimately, I achieved the Xerox President's Club distinction. That award paid off in numerous career opportunities further down the road. Thank you Mr. Kearney!

Most importantly - what do you EXPECT?

Expect, Understand and Own the Positive Future!

This profound, but simple model
accelerates performance when applied to
problems, opportunities and relationships.

Create a universal language and culture
in your company to replicate success
and foster teamwork!

Here's how...

Prepare Your Team in a Low Risk Environment to *EXPECT LEADERSHIP*

One Model for the Entire Company

We live in an increasingly technical world. This can often lead to a disconnect in relationships between more technical and less technical work groups. The power of integrating one simple model for cross-functional communication is a unifying platform for internal communication.

One Model – Multiple Applications

Expect, Understand and Own the Positive Future! is a flexible model for solving problems and strengthening relationships. In our experience, linear thinkers such as programmers, accountants and engineers find it useful in strengthening relationships while resolving challenges. Relationship oriented individuals like sales professionals find it to be a comfortable framework for building trust and ensuring revenue growth. ***Expect, Understand and Own the Positive Future!*** is the essence of consultative selling.

One Model Where Everyone Wins

Expect, Understand and Own the Positive Future! *is a win-win approach to business.* As a result, individual *EXPECT LEADERSHIP Journals* have been modularized to address issues faced primarily in Business, Technology, Engineering, Logistics and Sales.

Additional *Moment of Truth* Exercises, Templates, Role Plays and Scorecards are presented in each of the individual *EXPECT LEADERSHIP Journals*.

Regardless of the field of specialty,
Leaders master the art of *Expect, Understand and Own the Positive Future!* through role plays and repetition.

These tools are available in each *EXPECT LEADERSHIP* Journal.

Sneak Preview

With every sample Moment of Truth scenario outlined, you are given a Sneak Preview of the upcoming dilemma.

Coming Up...

Scene 2: Weak Performance Reviews Bite Back!

In the next scene, you'll watch a common dilemma turn into a white knuckle Moment of Truth... for the Leader! Who is really in the hot seat? The Leader or his direct report? Watch closely.

You would think that the employee who is about to be reviewed would be a little nervous. Unfortunately, the manager is face to face with a serious internal struggle. Should he continue his prior behavior of conflict avoidance or amend his ways?

Keep in Mind:

This scene brings to light the importance of giving adequate thought and preparation to each Performance Review a leader will administer.

Principles like "Be Proactive", "Reinforce Transparency", and One" are foundational pillars in circumstances like these.

Experienced Leaders Know:

The Performance Review is a lazy trap for the careless man simply give an inflated score and inadequate feedback to a are staggeringly high.

Many a leader has lost his job and his leadership stature b behavior by his or her direct reports. What will happen her major turnaround opportunity!

One Model, Five Steps...
Expect, Understand and Own the Positive Future!

Your Weak Performance Reviews Bite Back Your Solution

#1 – EXPECT and communicate the ideal outcome.

#2 – UNDERSTAND the situation. Ask your colleagues what happened.

#3 – OWN the outcome.

#4 – Accelerate POSITIVE

#5 – Plan for the FUTURE

Compare Your Solution to Our Solution!

Your Weak Performance Reviews Bite Back
Our Solution

1 2 3 4 5

#1 – EXPECT and communicate the ideal outcome
- Each employee has a written synopsis of what s/he has done well
- Each employee has a written game plan for improving his/her performance
- Each employee achieve his/her goals and knows that s/he is superstar.

#2 – UNDERSTAND the situation. Ask your colleagues what happened.
- Meet with each employee
- Ask each person to share how they feel about their impact or team results

#3 – OWN the outcome. Demonstrate leadership:
- Thank each employee for their candid appraisal of their performance
- Apologize for having teams off lighten past PR opportunities for improvement

#4 – Accelerate POSITIVE leadership momentum
- Provide a strong confirmation of the good things s/he has done to date
- Frequently explain where s/he had fallen back expectations
- Commit to providing accurate, helpful and productive PRs in the future
- You may want to provide a blank PR in advance of the meeting to enable each person to gives a comprehensive and thoughtful response
- Ensure you maximize strengths and improvement opportunities

#5 – Plan for the FUTURE. Help others reach the ideal expectation.
- Provide a set of constructive recommendations for improvement
- Create a game plan for the recommended action items
- Specify a specific period of time in which s/he should achieve each objective
- Meet at a predetermined time in the future to measure his/her progress

---

SCENE 2

WEAK PERFORMA
REVIEWS BITE BA

---

3 Ways to Role Play
Improvise with creativity!

ACTOR A
In each role play, you are the leader.

Approach this employee with the intent to "Understand."

Ask your direct report how s/he believes his/her performance has impacted the results of the team.

Probe to find out what s/he feels could be improved.

1 →

ACTOR B
You are the direct report. Respond by claiming that you have done a fantastic job for the team again this year.

State your excitement to hear what type of salary increase you'll receive as a result of two years of stellar performance results.

Ignore any shortcomings the leader may raise.

2 →

ACTOR B
You are the direct report. Answer any questions with responses like, "I really haven't given it much thought. After all, last year it seemed like this process was a mere formality."

Ask the leader if anything has changed from his perspective.

3 →

ACTOR B
Respond by acknowledging your strengths and one weakness.

Allow the leader to lead the conversation until s/he begins to suggest that other things could have also been better. Listen for specifics and ANGRILY challenge each one.

No matter how tough your conversation starts out... Expect Understand and Own the Positive Future!

- Executive Edition -
8

Weak Performance Reviews Bite Back!
Scene 1

nce review packet to your direct reports. You asked each employee of thought-provoking questions regarding their own performance.

ee to list:
ost significant accomplishments.
they fell short.
mprovement step they can take immediately.

e you know each person had some good things to document. On o know there are areas in each person's performance where they

Challenge:

Historically, you've felt you should be upbeat with every employee despite their performance. As a result, you've avoided discussing the tough issues. You realize the prior review process wasn't as helpful as it could have been. In addition, you didn't address several issues because you would have been uncomfortable discussing negative topics.

Today is the day you provide feedback to your team. Your first direct report comes into your office for feedback. His performance is okay, but not great. You're thinking about the need for candor as he enters.

Key Question:

As a manager, how will you handle this situation?

After you review each scenario, collaborate with your team to solve the real-world Challenge using Expect, Understand and Own the Positive Future!

Next Steps

EXPECT LEADERSHIP and turbocharge every level of your company.

Here are some powerful options to start today:

Train your Corporate Trainers
- Engage Keith Martino Leadership to equip your internal training experts to implement this model and strengthen your EXPECT LEADERSHIP culture.

Request Training Onsite
- Engage Keith Martino Leadership experts to provide *EXPECT LEADERSHIP* training to your team.

Request One-on-One Coaching
- Engage Keith Martino Leadership professionals to provide the proven *EXPECT LEADERSHIP* one-on-one coaching to specific managers.

Request Customized Support
- Invite Keith Martino Leadership to customize an *EXPECT LEADERSHIP* initiative for your company.

Order EXPECT LEADERSHIP Journals for your Team
- Order *EXPECT LEADERSHIP Training Journals* for your aspiring leaders. Targeted *EXPECT LEADERSHIP Journals* are available for Business, Technology, Engineering, Logistics and Sales.

Visit KeithMartino.com for more information.

PRICELESS ADVICE FOR BUSINESS LEADERS

Leadership is the ability to positively influence others. Practice leadership daily!

Engage every employee in delivering excellent customer service.

Accelerate your lead over your competition. Help colleagues see "the big picture."

Demonstrate daily the unique values and principles that guide your company.

Equip colleagues to recognize the problems they can solve at their own level.

Rise to the occasion in times of turbulence and uncertainty.

Show individual consideration. Recognize each employee's unique talents.

Help teammates achieve their unrealized potential.

Invest in your friends, family and colleagues.

Practice the relentless pursuit of excellence. Reward those who achieve it.

Expect
A better outcome than if the problem had never occurred.

Understand
Ask open-ended questions. Understand perceptions.

and Own
Take ownership by apologizing or thanking others.

the Positive
Remain positive... as a matter of principle!

Future
Create a plan and make it happen!

EXPECT, UNDERSTAND and *OWN* the *POSITIVE FUTURE!*

1. Refocus your team on the ideal outcome of a crisis or calamity.

2. Encourage each person to ask the right questions and listen.

3. Enhance camaraderie by thanking or apologizing as appropriate.

4. Interject your core values into the midst of the discussion.

5. Point your team towards a planning process that yields results.

EXPECT LEADERSHIP

Epilogue

We invite you to consider a few closing thoughts.

Embrace The Golden Rule
You now have a solid, simple model for turning goof-ups into gold. Anyone's goof-ups? Yes, including yours!

Expect, Understand and Own the Positive Future! will make you and your colleagues a bright light at the office and in the global marketplace. It will enable you to illuminate and impact the most troublesome catastrophes. Why? The foundation is the Golden Rule – "Treat others as you would like to be treated." Stated succinctly thousands of years ago, it's relevant today.

The Golden Rule builds trust. Trust is the cornerstone of every solid relationship.

You will become a catalyst for trust at all levels of your company when you practice this simple truth. And despite all misperceptions to the contrary, TRUST is the most valuable currency in your corporate treasury. Without trust there is no hope. Without trust, there is no team. Without trust, there is no long term customer relationship. Therefore, earning and strengthening trust is mission critical. *Expect, Understand and Own the Positive Future!*

Try It Up Close and Personal
Expect, Understand and Own the Positive Future! is even more rewarding when we regularly apply it in our personal relationships. Imagine the impact on loved ones.

Begin every difficult conversation with friends and family with high expectations. Establish a realistic desired outcome that your relationships will be stronger than ever as a result of the current dilemma you face. Consider the welcomed surprise as you seek to understand each person's perspective instead of driving home your own agenda.

Don't be stunned. Tears of joy may flow when you take ownership by sincerely apologizing for the role you played in the current catastrophe. Extend a heartfelt "thanks" to a peer and watch it brighten their day. Keep the faith and remind your loved ones of the encouragement that comes with a positive attitude. And finally, shape the future by clarifying who will take responsibility for each action item with dates for completion.

Never Give Up. Be relentless in your pursuit of the ideal outcome.
Follow-up is essential. The most complex *Moments of Truth* often require a complete repeat of the five step process to achieve the end goal. That's okay. Don't skip a single step when you repeat the process. 1-2-3-4-5. Each step will yield even greater clarity and confidence as you follow the model to success.

Expect, Understand and Own the Positive Future!

Acknowledgements

The following individuals and leaders have contributed to the success of specific EXPECT LEADERSHIP Journals.

Their accomplishments are documented in the following areas of specialization:

- Association Management
- Engineering
- Executive Management
- Financial Services
- Foreign Service
- Government
- Information Technology
- Logistics
- Marketing
- Ministry
- Project Management
- Sales Management

Acknowledgements

For Contributors to Targeted *EXPECT LEADERSHIP* Journals

If you have not yet picked up a copy of the Leadership Journal, you should. And then you'll know why these professionals' contributions have been so important.

Words will never fully express my heartfelt appreciation to those of you who have helped us complete this series of *Leadership Journals*. Many of you served in an important consulting capacity and each of you has challenged and encouraged us through your presence. I've outlined a tiny portion of your valuable insight below:

Business Journal

- Thanks to **Aaron C. Davis, MBA and Director at Touch Bionics**. You helped us rethink the executive summary, revisit the topic of what does "better off than if it hadn't occurred" really mean and you reminded us of the diversity of the readers who will benefit from this book. Thanks my man!

- Thanks to **Blair (Garner) Green, Chapter President at HSMAI**. You challenged us to make Dirk earn his keep or you threatened to "cut him lose." Dirk is better for the raised expectation. So are we! Thanks Blair!

- Thanks to **Gregory Fine, CAE, Chief Executive Officer at Turnaround Management Association**. You were instrumental in us writing the introduction and your encouragement to heighten the focus on the model was encouraging. And your wordsmithing was most appreciated. Thanks again Greg!

- Thanks to **Thomas R. Oliver, Chairman & CEO Emeritus, InterContinental Hotels Group**. Your positive influence over the past three decades has provided an ongoing stream of insight into the nature of leadership. In this particular endeavor, your focus on the simplicity and potential of the model brought out the discretionary effort in me. You still know how to inspire us just as you did at FedEx! Thanks for another fine memory!

Engineering Journal

- Thanks to **Marshall Chapman, Sales Engineer at LENZE**. Your sense of humor and encouragement to go beyond our present format gives us some great market opportunities to shoot for in the future. In addition, your reminder that we are all Dirk on any given day helped us rethink his potential as a leader. Thanks MC!

- Thanks to **Michael Miller, Chief Operating Officer at The ESCO Group**. You inspired us to write the *Journal Users Guide* to explain how to maximize the use of the book. Great suggestion! Your vision for how engineers would see this as a "process book" that never mentions that "A" word was extremely helpful. Thanks Mike!

Logistics Journal

- Thanks to **Brett Eifler, Branch President at XPO Logistics, Inc.** for reminding us of how critical the customer facing *Moment of Truth* experiences can be. You were sensitive to the value of the model in our personal lives as well. As a result, we emphasized it again in the Epilogue. Thanks Brett!

- Thanks to **Richard Metzler, Chief Marketing Officer at uShip.com.** Our long relationship remains an inspiration and in this endeavor (of which we've had a few... smile) you were the reason we added the scoring opportunity to the *Moment of Truth* exercises. Once again you helped us improve the product. Thanks Dick!

- Thanks to **Steve Thebeau, Regional Vice President at Roadrunner Transportation Services.** You reminded us of the importance of revisiting the status of the scenario later to ensure the *Moment of Truth* had truly moved forward. As a result, we included this in the closing Epilogue. Great reminder. Thanks Steve!

Technology Journal

- Thanks to **Robin Kennedy, Vice President at CB Technologies, Inc.** Your encouragement landed on a weekend when we were struggling to get past a significant hurdle. Your reminder of how the book scales up and down the organizational chart was just what we needed to keep working. Thanks again Robin!

- Thanks to **Susan (Alsobrook) Kennedy, President PMI Dallas.** Thanks to you and your husband for reminding us how influential Dirk can be when he gives his best. Your suggestions were integrated all the way down to the last exclamation point... smile. Thanks so much for your passion for the work!

- Thanks to **Thomas Martucci, Vice President at Consolidated Chassis Management, LLC.** How many people take a manuscript with them on their vacation?...smile. We really appreciated your insight and your reminder that there could be multiple outcomes using the model based on a person's expectations. As a result of your suggestions, we went back and repositioned how the principles tied to the model. Great idea!

And That's Not All

I've learned every successful leader has at least one mentor or trusted counselor in their life. In addition to the thought-leading professionals listed up to this point, there were others who simply never left the scene as we were writing this series. Their influence and leadership advice was so profound that I couldn't separate their thoughts from my own because they have impacted our work in so many ways:

- Thanks to **Beth Ellyn Rosenthal, Real Estate Mogul and Writer Extraordinaire.** Thanks for twenty-five years as our primary editor. I've appreciated every notation you've added. I would highly recommend your services to anyone who is considering putting their ideas or story on paper. You are an extraordinary person!

- Thanks to **Gregory W. Hext, CEO Chapman Hext & Co., P.C.** Your unbridled optimism and quest for excellence continuously challenges me to think and grow. Your invitation to apply the model in your business development process was a timely impetus for our future endeavors. Thanks for your friendship and support.

- Thanks to **Jerry Smith, President of The Cates Companies**. You were always on my mind as we put together the model and the *Moment of Truth* scenarios. Your willingness to provide a laboratory of real world opportunities spanning a decade plus of leadership work together inspired every page. Thanks my brother!

- Thanks to **Lane T. Cubstead, Retired Foreign Service Officer, U.S. Department of State**. Your challenging questions and endless quality checks on the consistency of our work was instrumental in our ability to complete this *Journal*. Your friendship is indispensable. Thanks Lane!

- Thanks to **Lisa DeSpain, Owner at Ebook Converting**. You were a bright ray of sunshine that came into our midst, and we're so glad you did. Your help in preparing this *Journal* for print and Ebook enabled us to leap any hurdle we encountered technically. Thanks for great layout suggestions and strategic guidance!

- Thanks to **Mark Villareal, Senior Vice President at Five Point Enterprises**. Your countless phone conversations and steady encouragement across a decade of time paved the way for this latest work. And your simple phrase... "Shortcuts Get You Lost" will never be forgotten. Thanks for your perseverance!

- Thanks to **Michelle Ingle, Graphic Designer**. You "worked on Dirk" to give him an amazing face-lift to match his charming personality. Your artistic interpretation inspired many of his quips and thoughts – which are alive and well inside many an organization. Thanks, Michelle, for helping bring Dirk to life!

- Thanks to **Eddy Ketchersid, Author and Minister** for a model to live by. Your example has become my benchmark for leadership in the eternal priorities of life. I'll spend the rest of my life trying to reach your level of success as a leader of men. Thanks for twenty-five years of mentoring and prayer.

And many more... friends and clients like Bradford Beldon, Doug Tyrrell, James Bowes, Jr., Julie Kelly, Lynn Bryant, Marty Carney, Michael D. Beldon, Rauline Ochs, Ray Ramu, Dr. Ray Taylor, Mr. and Mrs. Val Martino, and others we have not mentioned demonstrated the kind of leadership that sparked ideas and modeled success. And of course, Frederick W. Smith, leader of leaders who I still marvel at daily. The FedEx influence is pervasive in my life and work.

There are four people who have the most profound influence on all areas my personal, business and spiritual life. These ladies have given their all to enable this *Journal* to become a possibility and then a reality. First, **Terri Martino**, my wife of thirty-four years. Terri serves as Chief Benevolence Officer at College Market Institute. Without Terri my world stops. Secondly, **Olivia Martino**, who puts the smile in our lives and models the true essence of love. **Laura Martino**, whose fingerprints are on every page and every picture. Thank you beyond words Laura! And of course, **Melody Martino** the catalyst of all things fresh, new and different. My name on the front of the book is shorthand for these ladies who did it.

But most of all, I give thanks to our God, the Rock of Ages, the Sustainer of Life and the Author of all that is good. God's mercies are fresh each morning.

ABOUT THE AUTHOR

Keith Martino has a passion for helping motivated leaders deliver results.

Martino is head of **CMI**, a global consultancy founded in 1999 that customizes leadership and sales development initiatives. Recent CMI partnerships include the creation and expansion of the *Oracle Partner Leadership Program* for North America and Eastern Europe. In addition, CMI helped launch the *Safeco Insurance Leadership Acceleration Program* and the *Cates/I2R Leadership Institute*. CMI also provides leadership assessment support for the Verizon Product Showcase.

After more than 20 years and numerous awards at FedEx, Xerox and Baxter Healthcare, Martino's team provides world-class counsel and proven web-based tools that produce consistent results. His team delivers assessments, training and one-on-one performance coaching. CMI Leadership assessments are available in English, German, Turkish, and Russian.

Martino has been the keynote speaker at business development conferences for Xerox, Bass Pro Shops, New Horizons Computer Learning Centers, The American Banking Association, Baker-Hughes, Shell Oil, RadioShack, Schlumberger, and others. He has consulted clients in the fields of telecommunications, business intelligence, computer integration services, healthcare, financial services, education, and strategic planning among others.

Martino has led sales and marketing organizations throughout his career. His group was twice recognized as the top global accounts team in the world for FedEx.

Leadership books in the *EXPECT LEADERSHIP* series by Keith Martino include:

- *EXPECT LEADERSHIP - The Executive Edition*
- *EXPECT LEADERSHIP in Business*
- *EXPECT LEADERSHIP in Engineering*
- *EXPECT LEADERSHIP in Logistics*
- *EXPECT LEADERSHIP in Sales*
- *EXPECT LEADERSHIP in Technology*

Martino has published three sales handbooks entitled **Get Results** and **Results Now**. His international handbook, **Selling to Americans** is available globally via E-delivery. For more information on Keith Martino visit www.KeithMartino.com.

www.ingramcontent.com/pod-product-compliance
Lightning Source LLC
Chambersburg PA
CBHW081555220326
41598CB00036B/6687